10 Hikes in Harriman Park and More

10 Hikes in Harriman Park and More

1 Day Vacations

Paul Huberman

iUniverse, Inc.
New York Lincoln Shanghai

10 Hikes in Harriman Park and More
1 Day Vacations

iUniverse books may be ordered through booksellers or by contacting:

iUniverse
2021 Pine Lake Road, Suite 100
Lincoln, NE 68512
www.iuniverse.com
1-800-Authors (1-800-288-4677)

The views expressed in this work are solely those of the author and do not necessarily reflect the views of the publisher, and the publisher hereby disclaims any responsibility for them.

ISBN-13: 978-0-595-42100-8 (pbk)
ISBN-13: 978-0-595-86443-0 (ebk)
ISBN-10: 0-595-42100-8 (pbk)
ISBN-10: 0-595-86443-0 (ebk)

Printed in the United States of America

TABLE OF CONTENTS

INTRODUCTION

At least once a week since 1989 on average, I've visited Harriman State Park in Rockland County, NY, either to hike, fish, or take pictures. Over time, I learned that the preserve was like The Bible or a symphony: the deeper you looked, the more you saw and appreciated. It amazed me that the Park, considering its many positive attributes, was not more heavily visited despite its proximity to New York City. Weigh these facts about the Harriman Park and its smaller, adjacent companion Bear Mountain State Park and see if you don't agree: (1) the forest ranks as New York's second largest park with over 50,000 acres; (2) Harriman is a nearly 100% pure or non-fragmented wilderness with few roads or signs of civilization; (3) the Park is only a 45 minute drive from the Upper West Side of Manhattan; (4) the forest is water-rich with an abundance of lakes and streams; (5) Harriman's geology is especially varied and complex; and (6) in the same way that a house retains the feel of its previous occupants, traces of generosity can still be felt related to the Harriman family's gift of land in the early part of the 1900s to form the Park.

To my way of thinking, Harriman Park isn't a crowded, rundown forest that has seen better days. It's a roughly 5 mile by 15-mile patch of New England forest that was somehow air lifted from Vermont and deposited in southern New York! Instead of driving 6 hours to get a totally refreshing experience, you only have to drive 45 minutes. Based on field and anecdotal evidence, I believe hiking is an under appreciated activity among New Yorkers. If someone were to perform a statistical analysis of the number of visitors per acre to the Blue Hills or Middlesex Fells reservations near Boston and compare it to Harriman State Park, I am sure the evidence would show that hiking is a much more popular among New England residents. The same outcome would probably also apply for parks near other major metropolitan areas such as Philadelphia, Pittsburgh or Chicago. New York's emphasis on "indoor culture" such as art museums, plays, concerts and the like probably explains part of this phenomenon. A second reason is that many city and borough residents don't own a car. New York bore the brunt of the 9-11 terrorist attacks. Even today the terror alert for the city is elevated—higher than for the nation as a whole. One place that offers solace along with recreational opportunities and is virtually free is nearby Harriman State Park.

My goal is to inspire this "silent majority" or "untapped market" of potential outdoor enthusiasts to hike in Harriman Park. The three illustrated maps are a direct attempt to reach this audience. Seeing images of George Washington, a scrub brush denoting a smooth rock surface, a waterfall, or an iron mine must surely excite wanderlust in even the most die-hard city dweller. Moreover, the 10 mostly moderate hikes profiled in the book were distilled from a large universe of possibilities and selected because they offer interesting attractions or particular scenic beauty. For the novice and the experienced hiker, this book utilizes an interval or "sum of the parts" approach that breaks each hike down into short manageable stretches. It should be readable and easy to follow. Finally, I've cheated a little, recommending non-outdoor lures, such as a nourishing chicken soup at a nearby Mexican restaurant or a classic turn of the century movie theatre. The intent is to enhance the hiking experience by making it part of an entire day of enjoyable activities.

The author wishes to thank the following individuals who either read parts of the book and offered helpful comments or who, more importantly, were wonderful companions in the woods: Jabril Bensedrine, Michael Belotz and Christine Bourgeois, Arnold Huberman, Linda Khachadurian, Susan Kosowiz, Bob Ligansky, Robert Murray, CFA, CMA, Michael and Janice Peran, Lauren Sacks, Fred Rassi, Ellie Richard, Pam Tong, and David Zeven.

My mood on August 15, 2005 was beatific, a result of exercise, fresh air, open space, and a delicious dinner. The sun set in the dip between two hills and an orange glow filled the sky. I couldn't wait to go again. Do you want to join me?

WHERE IS HARRIMAN STATE PARK
AND BEAR MOUNTAIN?

The answer to this question seven different ways, several of which should suffice depending on where you live are: 45 miles north of Manhattan next to the Hudson River; a few miles south of the West Point Military Academy; in Rockland County, NY; several miles north of Mahwah, NJ in Bergen County; opposite the Hudson River from Croton-On-The-Hudson in Westchester County; very close to exit 15A on the New York Thruway; five miles east of Greenwood Lake in New Jersey; and on either side of the Palisades Interstate Parkway at about the 20 mile mark from its start near Fort Fee, NJ. If you consult a map, Harriman Park and Bear Mountain (really the same forest but distinct for naming purposes) will appear as the largest patch of green anywhere near New York City, far larger than Prospect Park in Brooklyn. The major roads that run through or near the Park are Highway 17, the New York Thruway, the Palisades Interstate Parkway, and in the Park itself, Seven Lakes Drive.

HOW TO DECIDE WHICH HIKE IS RIGHT FOR YOU

Assuming you've arrived at Harriman State Park, the next decision is which hike to go on. If you are a first-time visitor, try the Tourist Hike. It starts from a central location you can't miss, the Visitor Center on Seven Lakes Dr., is of moderate difficulty, and features a number of interesting historical or scenic attractions. Hiking with young children? Then try The View. About half this short hike is along a woods road, and the view of Lake Stahahe is sure to please. Want to go straight to the top quality wise? In that case, I recommend The Sky Hike. This route passes some of Harriman's most spectacular scenery, including glacial carvings and three incredible overlooks. Be sure to take a camera. Do you find mountain lakes relaxing? If so, Land and Lake is your hike. This route passes three bodies of water and has a nice inland stretch for balance. Interested in history? A Hill, History and A Hamlet on the Bear Mountain side of the Park allows you to tour a historic hamlet and walk on the trail a British General used during the Revolutionary War. An added feature on the route is three to four picturesque waterfalls, including one the locals called "Ten Foot." Love to hike but worry about getting lost. If you fit this description, then try Twin Peaks. There are only three trails or roads you need to follow and they are clearly marked. The risk of getting lost is quite low. Finally, do you like a challenge? If so, The Himalayan Trek fits the bill. This outing is rated difficult minus. From the trailhead it takes about an hour and 45 minutes of solid hiking to reach the Timp Cliff. Along the way you'll need to scale 1,100 ft. high West Mountain and then another 300 feet to the top of the Timp. This is nearly a full day outing.

HITTING THE HIGHLIGHTS

While the choices given below are to a certain extent subjective, they represent the author's best guesses as to what spots you would most enjoy. Two of the five best views are of the Hudson River. The number two waterfall is actually mountain run off and not stream-based and therefore only viewable after a downpour.

BEST SCENIC OVERLOOKS

1. The Hudson River from the top of Bald Mountain on the red (Ramapo Dunderberg) trail in quadrant F3 of the Trail Conference's Harriman Bear Mountain Trails, northern map. Hike reference: A Hill, History and a Hamlet.

2. Lake Kanawauke from the * on the red (Arden Surebridge) trail in quadrant C4 of the Trail Conference's Harriman Bear Mountain Trails, southern map. Hike Reference: The Sky Hike.

3. Lake Stahahe from Stahahe Peak in quadrant B4 on an unmarked trail in the Trail Conference's Harriman Bear Mountain Trails, southern map. See THE VIEW.

4. The Hudson River from the red (Ramapo Dunderberg) trail on West Mountain in quadrant E3 of the Trail Conference's Harriman Bear Mountain Trails, northern map. Hike reference: A Himalayan Trek.

5. Lake Sebago from the blue (Seven Hills) trail in quadrant B5 of the Trail Conference's Harriman Bear Mountain Trails, southern map. Hike reference: Tasting High Country.

MOST PEACEFUL SPOTS

1. Parker Cabin Mountain on the red (Ramapo Dunderberg) trail in quadrant B4 of the Trail Conference's Harriman Bear Mountain Trails, southern map. Not discussed in book.

2. Flat lakeside trail (unmarked) by third reservoir in quadrant C5 of the Trail Conference's Harriman Bear Mountain Trails, southern map. Hike Reference: Land and Lake

3. Bridge over stream on the blue (Long Path) trail in quadrant C4 Trail Conference's Harriman Bear Mountain Trails, southern edition. Hike Reference: Land and Lake.

4. Stream on the blue (Seven Hills) trail in quadrant A6 of the Trail Conference's Harriman Bear Mountain Trails, southern edition. Hike Reference: The Wonders of Nature.

5. Your choice.

MOST SPECTACULAR WATERFALLS

1. Tuxedo Falls, which splits into two main cascades, can be seen by walking about one half mile north from the train station in Tuxedo. There is also the Augusta Iron Furnace about 70 ft. from the falls.

2. The 15-ft free fall cascade about 3.5 miles west of the Tiorati Circle on Arden Valley Rd. in quadrant C3 of the northern edition of the map set is formed by run off and is therefore seasonal. Late October is usually a good time to see it.

3. Ten Foot near Doodletown in quadrant F2 of the northern map. Hike Reference: A Hill History and A Hamlet.

4. The Waterslide behind the meadow from Lake Wanoksink on Pine Meadow Road in quadrant C5 and B5 of the southern map. Hike Reference: Tasting High Country.

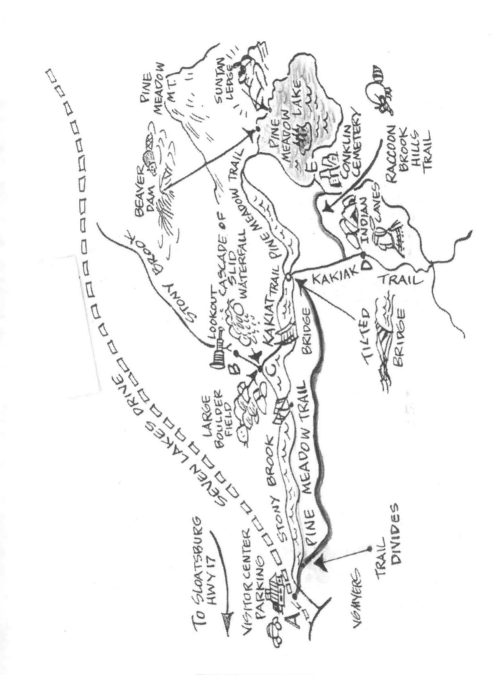

THE TOURIST HIKE

THE TOURIST HIKE

Distance: 5.5 miles
Time: 2.5 hours
Difficulty Level: Moderate
Map: Harriman Bear Mountain Trails, southern, quadrants A5 and B5

Pros: easy to find trailhead, well traveled, beaver dam, beautiful lookout, old cemetery, Indian caves, small scenic waterfall.

Cons: may be crowded, sometimes difficult to follow trail.

Guiding Markers: Stony Creek, Cascade of Slid Waterfall, wood bridge, Ga-Nus-Quah Rocks, Indian Caves, Pine Meadow Lake, Old cemetery.

Directions to trailhead: From the intersection of Highway 17 in Sloatsburg and Seven Lakes Dr., proceed 1.5 miles east to the Visitor Center on the right.

DESCRIPTION

The 5.5-mile hike, perhaps the best introduction to Harriman Park, packs in five scenic, historical or naturalistic attractions, more than any other trek I know of. By chance, three of the major attractions-the waterfall, the Indian Caves, and the cemetery, are spaced almost exactly 30 minutes apart. An over-simplified way to visualize the trek is to image yourself following a stream to its source, Pine Meadow Lake.

ROUTE PLAN AND MARKING POSTS

Point A-Visitor Center
Point B-Cascade of Slid Waterfall

From the Visitor Center on Seven Lakes Dr. head into the forest and walk along Stony Brook. At first, you'll be on the red (Pine Meadow) trail and then, the yellow (Stony Brook) path. The change in trails is almost irrelevant since you'll be hugging the stream for the entire stretch. In about 20 minutes you'll reach the second of two wood bridges. This is the point where you can't go any further and the stream forks. Cross over, and turn right on the white trail (Kakiat) into a boulder filled area. From here, its 10 minutes to the Cascade of Slid Waterfall. This gushing waterfall comes off a large rock at an angle; a smaller chute can be seen to the left. A bridge is about 35 ft. away up the stream.

Point B-Cascade of Slid Waterfall
Point C-Indian Caves

Just above the Cascade of Slid Waterfall and across from the span bridge is a rock painted with white and orange blazes. For an optional detour to a nice view, take the orange trail (Hillburn-Tuxedo-Sloatsburg) up a steep hill for five minutes to arrive at a nice lookout. The panorama is telescopic, as the bordering mountains channel your view down toward the Visitors Center. Then, retrace your steps back the hill to the stream and turn left up Pine Meadow Brook. After 10 minutes of mostly flat terrain, you'll reach a wood bridge, which was once damaged by beavers. Go across the bridge, turn left and continue for 20 minutes on the white trail up a moderately steep grade to the black (Raccoon Brook Hills) trail. Turn left onto the black-blazed trail and in about 100 yards you'll see the Indian Caves. The inhabitants of this formation, which to my mind resembles Stonehenge, were probably the Lenapi Indians.

Segment C-Indian Caves
Point D-Conklin Cemetery

Continue on the black (Raccoon Brook Hills) trail to a hill with a good but partly obstructed view, eventually reaching the stub of the yellow trail. The yellow trail ends at a dirt road on the edge of Pine Meadow Lake. Once there, turn right and proceed about 50 yards up a small hill and stop. Try to visually orient to the graveyard. Key identifier: the cemetery is across from an Island in Pine Meadow Lake and about 150 yards from where you are standing. There's no official route, but the trail closest to lakeside seems to work best even though you have to crash through some brush initially.

An eerie light illuminates these grounds. Don't linger long. The oldest stone, that of Ezekiel Conklin, dates to 1811. According the Harriman Trails by William Myles (an excellent and comprehensive book on Harriman Park), the Conklin's first settled in the area in 1724 and left in 1935. Pine Meadow Lake was built by the Civilian Conservation Corp. during the Great Depression in the 1930s.

Point D-Conklin Cemetery
Point A-Visitor Center

Return to the dirt road around Pine Meadow Lake, turn right and head towards a concrete dam at the west end of the lake. Notice two beaver dams on the other side on the lake to the left of the cliff. You may also see fish in the summer and possibly turtles, which can be quite large. On April 13, 2003, noontime visitors to the lake were treated to a fine performance by two ducks and a goose, which dove under the water, scooted on the surface, and squawked at each other.

For the final leg back, take the red (Pine Meadow) trail down the hill just behind the concrete dam back to the Visitor Center. The trail is actually a road at this point but narrows later. The return segment divides into two sections. In the first leg, which takes about 20 minutes, you'll pass Ga-Nus-Quah (stone giant) boulders and a natural bathtub like formation I call the "Jacuzzi" to arrive at the wood bridge you passed earlier. Cross the bridge and turn right. From here, its about 40 minutes of mostly downhill hiking to the trailhead. You'll be on the red trail the whole time.

Reaching the Cascade of Slid Waterfall on The Tourist Hike takes about 30 minutes from the trailhead.

I always thought that the rock complex used for shelter by the region's native inhabitants centuries ago resembled Stonehenge.

Conklin Family Cemetery by Pine Meadow Lake. The oldest headstone, that of Ezekiel Conklin, dates from 1811.

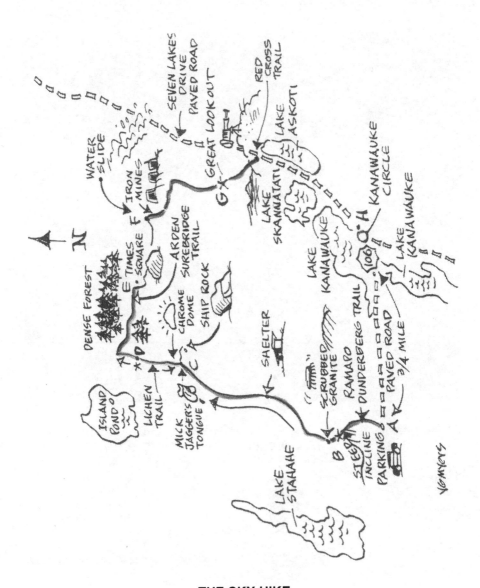

THE SKY HIKE

THE SKY HIKE

Distance: 6.2 miles
Time: 2 hours 45 minutes
Difficulty Level: Moderate
Map: Harriman Bear Mountain Trails, northern, quadrants B4, C3 and C4, and Illustrated Map.

Pros: three spectacular views, interesting glacial carvings, a rock that looks like a ship, old iron mines, photographic opportunities.

Cons: May require walking on the road for about 0.7 miles at the end, route is somewhat complex as it stitches together different trails.

Guiding Markers: the three lookouts, an overnight shelter, "Times Square," ship rock, the iron mines, Seven Lakes Drive.

Directions to Trailhead: From the intersection of Route 17 and Seven Lakes Drive in Sloatsburg, turn right on Seven Lakes Drive, go about 8 miles and turn left at the Kanawauke Circle. Then, proceed 1.8 miles, going past Little Long Pond and up a hill. Park on an unpaved area on the right side of the road. This spot is indicated by a P" on the Trail Conference map.

DESCRIPTION

Arguably Harriman's best hike, this trek passes especially breathtaking scenery: the overlooks of Lake Stahahe, Island Pond, and Lakes Skannatati and Kanawauke. These views are spread throughout the hike: at the 20-minute, one hour, and two hour marks. About 20% of the excursion is along the top of a ridge. You'll feel above it all, and see fascinating rock formations left by the receding glacier, including "Ship Rock." Other scenic attractions include a 45-foot water slide and mysterious flooded old iron mines. Bring your camera. Nature has perfectly framed the last lookout. Suggestion: Have some one in your group park at the Little Long Pond Parking Lot. Then, you can either end the hike or shuttle the rest of your group 0.7 miles back to the trailhead. This avoids a 20-minute walk along a narrow and busy road (Route 106). You can shorten the hike even further by stationing a driver at the Lake Skannatiti parking lot. Note that the illustrated map mistakenly places point H at Lake Kanawauke; it should be at the Little Long Pond Parking area.

ROUTE PLAN AND MARKING POSTS

Point A-Parking area off Route 106
Point B-View of Lake Stahahe

After crossing a small stream next to Route 106, the red trail (Ramapo Dunderberg) plunges into a brushy section before emerging into an open or bowl-like area, which marks the beginning of a vigorous 15-minute climb to the point marked on the Trail Conference map with a black star, indicating "lookout". This effort is well rewarded. The view from the flat granite ledge on top has a compelling and refreshing quality. You'll survey Lake Stahahe to the west and pure green hills to the west, north and south. A bench has been conveniently placed just below the summit if you want to rest. I've noticed that the people one meets here are unusually social, so be prepared to exchange greetings and for short conversations. Fun Fact to Know and Tell: Lake Stahahe is a natural body of water formed by glacial carvings; most of Harriman's other lakes were built by the Civilian Conservation Corp. during the Great Depression-1929-1940.

Point B-View of Lake Stahahe
Point C-Top of "Crome Dome"

Put it in cruise control for about 75% of this leg. You'll be on top of the ridge on a relatively flat trail in Quadrant B4 enjoying views in several directions. Because of this sections ease and beauty, this trek was originally entitled "The Elegant Hike." (In all fairness, there are a few challenging descents.) About one-quarter mile past the overnight shelter is a smooth-polished area called "whaleback." The illustrated map has a scrub brush at this point. Two more landmarks in the glacial erosion theme on the illustrated map: "Mick Jagger's Tongue," a smooth, ramp like area, followed almost immediately by "Crome Dome," a polished or abraded hill. Final exam quiz: can you spot the gravity defying rock nearby? At the top of Crome Dome (Point C) one detours 200 yards on the Ramapo-Dunderberg trail to Ship Rock, a 20-ft high rock shaped like the bow of a ship, before returning to the peak of the polished dome.

Point C-Top of "Crome Dome"
Point D-View of Island Pond

From the top of Crome Dome, one takes the Lichen (blue trail) a short distance to a nice view of Island Pond. One challenge on this section is a 3 ft. drop off. Tip: get down on your rear and go front-first. Estimated total hiking time from the trailhead to the view of the Island Pond: one hour.

Point D-View of Island Pond
Point E-Times Square

Leaving the exposed granite ridge near the Island Pond view (Point D), the trail then plunges steeply into a thick forest of fir trees. This sudden and delightful contrast in scenery heightens one's appreciation for the wonders of nature. Switchbacks on the blue trail make it hard to follow down the hill. Don't worry. Just keep descending and you will intersect with the jointly blazed blue/red trail, where the Arden Surebridge and Long Path trails run together. Follow this path for about 20 minutes, and then turn right on Surebridge Rd. to arrive at Times Square (Point E). Time Square, a large rock, derives its name from the convergence four tails, depending on how you count. Don't expect bright lights like the Manhattan's Times Square. In fact, the area is rather dark because of the tall trees block out much of the sun.

Point E-Times Square
Point F-Large Iron Mine next to waterslide

From Times Square (point E) head east and downhill on the Arden Surebridge trail, which is essentially a seven-foot wide rocky road. (I believe from actual experience that this trail is blazed a light green or blue although my edition of the map shows it as red). The key thing to remember is that you will be on a dirt road, not a narrow trail. After about 10 minutes you will reach an estimated 90-ft deep iron mine (Point F) bordered by a 45-ft. waterslide. A picture of this mine appears on later in this section. About four other less spectacular mines are near this excavation pit, all filled in with green water.

Point F-Large Iron Mine next to waterslide
Point G-View of Lake Kanawauke

From the iron mine "road," the red trail humps over two short, steep hills and a stream (where I once saw a fox) before climbing to the top of Pine Swamp mountain. Here, you are treated to the last and the best of the three great views. Straight ahead is Lake Kanawauke and to the left Lake Askoti. The Trail Conference map identifies this lookout with a black star. This vista would do Ansel Adams proud. Nature has perfectly framed it. Visit around mid October with a camera and you'll capture memorable colors. Lake Kanawauke will register as shimmering blue glass.

Point G-View of Lake Kanawauke
Point H-Parking area at Little Long Pond

You now return to civilization, descending on the red (Ramapo Dunderberg) trail past one tricky scramble to the Lake Skanatati Parking Lot. Just past the scramble is a large rectangular shaped rock about 3 feet wide and 10 feet long. (I have a macabre name for this rock: Frankenstein's coffin.) From the Lake Skannatati parking lot go up the hill to Seven Lakes Drive and turn right in the direction of Sloatsburg and the Lake Kanawauke Circle. At the circle turn right on Route 106 and continue past Lake Kanawauke to the Little Long Pond Parking area, if you are using the shuttle option or to the trailhead. This distance from Lake Skannatati to the parking area is about one mile.

Smooth granite surface polished by the glacier on The Sky Hike.

An unidentified person peers into a deep cavernous iron mine next to a 45 ft. waterslide (not shown).

This view of Lake Kanawauke is one the best overlooks in Harriman Park. An average person can take a professional quality picture here.

Canadian geese, big and small, can often be seen at the Lake
Kanawauke circle in mid May on clear days.

A HILL, HISTORY AND A HAMLET

A HILL, HISTORY AND A HAMLET

Distance: 5.5 miles
Time: 2 hours, 45 minutes
Difficulty Level: Moderate
Map: Harriman Trails Bear Mountain, quadrants F2 and F3 and Illustrated Map.

Pros: Wonderful waterfalls, an incredible view, local and Revolutionary War history, bird watching in nearby Iona Island.

Cons: challenging switchbacks before the summit of Bald Mountain, a steep stretch on the 1777 trail is often wet and slippery, brief sections on unmarked trails.

Guiding Markers: Timp Brook, waterfalls, switchbacks, the top of Bald Mountain, the Cornell mine, a fireplace, the Doodletown hamlet, a Reservoir, a 150-year old Oak tree, and a 200-year old Maple Tree

Directions to Trailhead: From the parking lot at the Bear Mountain Inn (where the bus drops off hikers) go out to the road, turn right, and at the circle head downhill to reach 9W/202. This road is essentially at sea level. Park on your left just after a small bridge on your right, about 100 yards north of the entrance to Iona Island.

DESCRIPTION

This gem of a hike offers three worthy waterfalls in the first half-mile, one of the Park's best views of the Hudson River, and a fascinating old settlement complete with cemeteries, a reservoir, and a 200-year old Maple tree. The return trip is on the 1777 trail, a path trod by British soldiers during the Revolutionary War. Afterwards, one can visit nearby Iona Island, a home to wintering eagles and numerous other bird species.

ROUTE PLAN AND MARKING POSTS

Point A-Parking Area on 9W
Point B-10 Ft. Waterfall

An omen of good things to come, the blue (Cornell Mine) trail begins at the base of a beautiful waterfall formed by The Timp Brook. This cascade is located 30-40 feet from the road. The trail initially climbs steeply to a plateau, levels out, and climbs again, establishing a pattern you will follow until the base of Bald Mountain. After about one-quarter of a mile, break off the blue trail to a path that parallels the Timp Brook. This move pays an immediate dividend: a delightful four-foot waterfall that plunges into a round pool. Just ahead is the more spectacular "Ten Foot," cascade, which splits into two major streams. Both cascades appear on the illustrated map. Don't worry about not being on a marked trail. You are basically paralleling the stream on this stretch.

Point B-10 Foot Waterfall
Point C-Top of Bald Mountain

From the 10 Foot waterfall, climb very steeply up the eastern hill, cross-country if necessary, to pick up the blue trail. It's not far away. You can also follow a road that begins at the top of Ten Foot. In about 20 minutes you will reach the base of Bald Mountain. A daunting task lies ahead: the ascent of the next 350 feet (estimated) via switchbacks. Always seeking new physical challenges, I was able to climb this stretch non-stop in 15 minutes; others sliced the time to 12 minutes. Remember: obstacles are short term, goals long term. Note that the illustrated mistakenly places the switchbacks near the Cornell Mine.

Once the switchbacks have been negotiated, turn right on the red (Ramapo-Dunderberg) trail for the remaining 40-foot climb to the summit. The view that waits on the summit of Bald Mountain is spectacular. I think it's the best in Bear Mountain State Park. You look almost straight north. The Hudson River appears like a blue snake wiggling back to Canada. A second attraction on top is the Cornell Mine, a cylindrical hole about 12 feet deep. Keep a safe distance. If you fall in, there appears to be an absence of handholds that could be used to climb out.

Point C-Top of Bald Mountain
Point D-Fireplace

For the next 15 minutes continue south along the red Ramapo-Dunderberg trail to a spot marked on the Trail Conference map as F for "Fireplace." Initially I thought the fireplace would be a brick kiln used to melt iron ore. It's actually a campfire grill for cooking hotdogs or hamburgers over charcoal.

Point D-Fireplace
Point E-Doodletown

From the Fireplace, turn right or west onto a woods road designated on the Trail Conference map as a series of broken dashes. At about the 0.4-mile-mark, the road ends, turning into the 1777 trail (red). Head right or north. This steep, mostly unpaved stretch can be slippery, so exercise proper caution. On a historical note, the 1777 trail one of the many paths the British, led by Sir Henry Clinton, traveled during the Revolutionary War. In about 30 minutes, you'll reach Doodletown, a settlement or hamlet founded in the 1760s and last occupied in 1965. The authoritative book on the subject is Doodletown: Hiking Through History in a Vanished Hamlet on the Hudson by Elizabeth Stalter. Various plaques that line the road offer a glimpse in the settlements history and residents: the Stalter home, a 200-year old maple tree, etc. There is a Park-supplied map for those who want to explore the June and Herbert cemeteries (although you will not be allowed to get too close), the reservoir, and various historical remains.

Point E-Doodletown
Point A-Parking area

From Doodletown, it's about one-half mile back to the trailhead. You'll initially follow the 1777e trail for about one-half mile, and then veer right onto a paved road (Timp Pass Road) that heads to 9W. Good trail sense is required at this point because you will be near the 1777e and 1777w trails and a road. However, don't worry about getting lost. You'll probably hear cars at this point.

Post hike, you may wish to visit Iona Island, one of four National Estuarine Reserves on the Hudson River, about 100 yards down the road. Besides eagles, which winter at this 560-acre marsh, other bird sightings include wood duck, American bittern, red-tailed hawk, belted kingfisher, prairie warbler, etc. Want to learn more about Iona Island? Here's a reference:

<http://www.nerrs.noaa. gov/HudsonRiver/IonaIsland.html> that describes
the site's plant life, endangered species, etc.

**The author will go on record as stating that he thinks this is the best
view in Harriman Park and Bear Mountain.**

This majestic waterfall (10 Foot) located near Doodletown splits into two major streams.

A HIMALAYAN TREK

Distance: 6.5 miles
Time: 3.5 Hours
Difficulty Level: Difficult Minus
Map: Harriman Bear Mountain Trails, northern, quadrant E3

Pros: Great work out, very nice Hudson River overlook, one trail covers 60% of the distance, Timp Cliff is spectacular.

Cons: Hard on knees, involves five different trails, route on top of West Mountain challenging to follow.

Guiding Markers: a signpost at about the 10-minute mark, a woods road, a view of the Hudson River from West Mountain, The Timp Cliff, large boulders at the base of The Timp

Directions to trailhead: From New York City, cross the George Washington Bridge and take the Palisades Interstate Parkway north to exit 17, Anthony Wayne Recreation area. Wend your way as far south as possible to the last parking lot. You will see picnic tables. Avoid signs that direct you back to the Palisades Interstate.

DESCRIPTION

This challenging up and back excursion to one of Bear Mountain's most prominent peaks involves a 700 foot climb, a 300 foot climb, and offers views of the Hudson River and Timp Cliff. Naturally, there is a chance to strengthen your quadriceps. Several small cliffs and pitch pines accent the downhill section from the top of West Mountain heading toward the Timp. I prefer this approach to The Timp over the route that starts from Highway 9W by the Hudson River; it avoids the view of the power plant and civilization.

ROUTE PLAN AND SEGMENT INTERVALS

Point A-South End of Anthony Wayne Parking Area
Point B-Sign Post

The first 10 minutes of this outing begins deceptively, with a casual stroll on a woods road through an early growth pine forest. You will cross two bridges before reaching a wood sign post at the intersection of the white (Appalachian Trail) trail and the road. The post lists hiking distances to various points.

Point B-Sign Post
Point C-Base of Red (Ramapo Dunderberg) Trail

You now embark on an "introductory climb," taking the white (Appalachian) trail uphill for 10 minutes and then turning right onto a wide unpaved road (Beechy Bottom Road) for a quarter of a mile to reach the red (Ramapo Dunderberg) trail. This brief ascent on the Appalachian trail serves an important purpose: it shaves 10% off the total climb to the top of West Mountain.

Point C-Base of Red (Ramapo Dunderberg) Trail
Point D-Base of Timp Cliff

This stretch, which covers 60% of the hike and takes about one hour, takes you to the top of West Mountain, across the top, and then down the other side. It divides into three phases: first, a very steep initial descent of about 700 ft. that takes about 35-40 minutes. If your legs complain, think of the nice view of the Hudson River ahead. And what a view it is, bold, impressive, capturing a wide swath of the river and further south, Manhattan. I think it's the fourth best panorama in the Harriman Park-Bear Mountain preserve. In the second leg, which takes about 10 minutes, the trail skirts the plateau of West Mountain across thick grass. The red blaze is faint or poorly marked. One trick to staying on the path is, paradoxically, to turn around and look back.

The third phase of the hike begins on the other side of West Mountain where, after a short, steep descent, you'll see the Timp Cliff towering in the east. I call this stretch, which takes about 20 minutes, "the traverse" because it slices across the mountain. You'll pass past several small cliffs and at one point it will be necessary to cross a fairly tricky lateral scramble. One nice feature of this stretch is that you can visually fix on the end destination quite easily. At the bottom of "the traverse" you will come upon a dirt road. Bear left for several hundred yards. After crossing a stream, turn right at the blue (Timp Torne) trail.

Point D-Base of Timp Cliff
Point E-Timp Summit

This leg of the outing along the blue trail (Timp Torne) climbs the remaining 300 ft. to the top of the 1,080 ft. Timp peak and takes about 20 minutes. There are lots of steps. Notice the large boulders at the base. Feel the mountain's presence, the aura of calm strength. Once on top, you are treated to rolling views of Harriman Park to the west and Perkins Tower to the north, with somewhat obstructed views of the Hudson River. Overnight campers may be seen in the bowl or depression just back from the cliff, which serves as a break against wind.

Points E-Timp Summit
Point A-South End of Anthony Wayne Parking Area

Retrace your steps. In about an hour and 45 minutes you will be back at the parking area. One subtlety in terminology: the traverse that you took going down is now best described as "the reverse."

The Timp Cliff on the "Himalayan Trek" looms large in the distance from the western approach via the stretch I call "the traverse."

This view of the Hudson River from West Mountain ranks as one the best in Bear Mountain.

THE VIEW

Distance: 3.5 miles
Time: 1.5 hours
Difficulty Level: Easy
Map: Harriman Bear Mountain Trails, northern, quadrant A4

Pros: Easy hike suitable for young children, modest elevation gain, unique view. Ice stalactites form in a gorge near the gate on Route 106. Detour to Boston Mine possible.

Cons: unmarked trail poorly blazed, lots of rocks at the beginning of Island Pond road compromise footing.

Guiding Markers: a gate near Route 106, Island Pond Rd., "Sugar Tooth" rock, view of Island Pond

Directions to trailhead: From the Kanawauke Circle on Seven Lakes Drive take Route 106 west past Little Long Pond and park at the second area marked with a "P" on the Trail Conference Map in quadrant B4. This will be on your left side and about 3.5 miles from the circle.

DESCRIPTION

This easy up and back outing suitable for hot summer days or groups with small children takes you to one of the most amazing views in Harriman Park, and possibly the east coast. From the top of Stahahe High Peak, Lake Stahahe appears both enlarged and far away. It feels like you are standing on top of the lake. Upon closer examination, you realize the lake is less than one mile away. It reminds me of a science fiction movie, or the larger than life view of Manhattan from Liberty State Park in Jersey City, NJ.

ROUTE PLAN AND MARKING POSTS

Point A-Parking area on Route 106
Point B-"Sugar Tooth" rock

Starting at the parking area, go across Route 106 and pick up a dirt trail that parallels 106 for several hundred yards to arrive at a gate and a stream. This is the beginning of Island Pond Rd. Take Island Pond Road for about one half a mile (generally bearing left when given a choice between roads) until you see a rock about six and half feet high shaped like an incisor tooth on your right. I call this glacial erratic "Sugar Tooth" rock. Across from this rock is the start of an unmarked blue-blazed trail shown on the trail conference map in broken dashes.

(If you're feeling adventurous, you can continue on Island Pond Rd. another one quarter mile to the Boston Mine on the right. This cavernous pit filled with green water is sure to amaze and entertain.)

Point B-"Sugar Tooth Rock"
Point C-Lake Stahahe Lookout

Follow the unmarked trail west about 0.4 miles, passing an open brushy area, a meadow on your right, and a section with several pools (assuming its rained recently) before reaching a steep 15-20 ft. climb. Here, **do not** follow the wider path to the right, which looks like a road, but go straight up the narrower trail past three rocks. Once on top, turn left along the backside of the plateau. In about 10 minutes you will reach the lookout. Take my word for it: this view is captivating.

Point C-Lake Stahahe Lookout
Point A-Parking area on Route 106

Retrace your steps to conclude the hike.

In the winter, ice stalactites or daggers form in the six-foot gorge carved by the stream just down from the gate. It's worth a visit to see the sharp teeth lining this mini Grand Canyon.

This amazing view of Lake Stahahe hits you immediately. The lake looks much bigger and further away than it really is.

Believe it or not, the deer in this spontaneous photo was actually eating a cold bagel.

DOCTORS AND LAWYERS

DISTANCE: 5.5 miles
TIME 2.5 hours
DIFFICULTY LEVEL: Moderate
MAP: Harriman Park Bear Mountain Trails, southern, quadrant B5

Pros: Local history, nice views from Claudius Smith's Den and the almost perpendicular summit, good parking at Johnsontown road, generally well-cleared paths with virtually no bush whacking, neat bowl-like (or amphitheatre) area about half way between Claudius Smith's den and almost perpendicular.

Cons: Car noise from Seven Lakes Dr. on the first leg, certain spots flooded after a rain.

Guiding Markers: Seven Lakes Dr., the point where the White Bar trail turns into a woods road, the cellar entrance, a row of cliffs, Claudius Smiths Den, a mine, a bowl-like area just before a star on the blue disc trail the lookout of the Visitor Center.

Directions to Trailhead: From the intersection of Route 17 and Seven Lakes Dr., follow Seven Lakes Drive east 0.3 miles, turn left, and then make a quick right on Johnsontown Rd. Proceed several miles to the end and park at the circle marked with a "P" in Quadrant A5 on the Trail Conference's Southern Map.

DESCRIPTION

This hikes features two historical attractions of a legal and medical nature for the upwardly mobile: a cave or den used by a bandit in the late 1700s, and the remains of an herb doctor's house dating from the late 1800s. The view from the summit of Claudius Smith's den is very good; the view from the top of the "almost perpendicular" lookout, while not as impressive, is still good. The route's overall pattern looks like a square with four main legs of roughly equal length set at 90-degree angles to each other.

Point A-Johnsontown Road Circle Parking Area
Point B-Dutch Doctor Cellar

From the Johnsontown Road circle follow the white (White Bar) trail for about 1.5 miles or 30 minutes to the remains of the Dutch Doctor's cellar entrance. This route generally parallels Seven Lakes Dr. Car noise is a detraction; other the other hand, you almost certainly won't get lost. About halfway to point B the trail widens into a dirt road. Finding the cellar, which looks like the remains of a chimney, isn't hard. It's about five feet from the road on your left and measures 8 ft. wide and 2.5 ft. high at its highest point. It's made of rocks cobbled together as if they were bricks. On the theory that less is more, I would stop here as far as directions. But more technically, the cellar is sandwiched between the second tree with a red blaze (indicating the start of the Tuxedo Mt. Ivy Trail) on your left and the road (White Bar Trail). If you see the overnight shelter on your right, you've gone about 150 yards too far. I have not been able to determine what herbs Dr. Wagner grew or if he graduated from an accredited medical school. William Myles says that the house was abandoned around 1900.

Point B-Dutch Doctor Cellar
Point C-Claudius Smith's Den

Turn left or west on the red (Tuxedo Mt. Ivy) trail and continue for about 0.75 miles or 25 minutes. The main features of this stretch include, in this order, a small to medium-sized hill, a wall of 12 to 15-ft. high cliffs on your right, and a meadow that explodes with colors in the fall. In the summer of 2002, I came across a bird's nest with eggs at the base of one of the cliffs. The finding was a surprise since at that height it would appear that a snake or other predator could have easily raided the eggs. The view from the top of Claudius Smith's Den is quite nice. The panorama stretches from southwest to north. Be careful; the crag drops off sharply. I'd estimate the drop at 75 ft. Claudius Smith's Den is a popular spot. You may encounter rock climbers, campers, and photographers.

The den itself contains two main chambers. At ground level you'll see an overhang and the remains of a fire. This was where Claudius' gang kept their horses. The narrower upper chamber, most accessible from the side of the cliff, was where the men slept. After a nefarious career that included stints as a robber and murder, Claudius Smith was put to death in Orange County (Goshen) in January 1779.

Point C-Claudius Smith's Den
Point D-Almost Perpendicular Lookout

Walk down from the cliff and head south to pick up the blue (Blue Disc) trail. Highlights of this leg are a mine (not shown on the map), a close squeeze by a cliff (indicated as "elbow brush" on the map) and just before the star (*) near Pound Mountain on the map, a descent into bowl-like or amphitheatre-like area. One interesting formation you'll pass before descending to the bowl is a "rock closet," a squarish area about 8 ft high on each side and 4 ft. wide, on your left.

I once surprised a turkey vulture resting in this enclosed space. The animal took off in a rush. The commotion was like a helicopter lifting off.

From the almost perpendicular lookout (Quadrant A5), you can see the Visitor Center on Seven Lakes Dr. Sunsets to the west are quite nice from this vantage point.

Point D-Almost Perpendicular Lookout
Point A-Johnsontown Road Circle Parking Area

This 0.75-mile stretch involves a steep initial descent of about 25 ft., a stream crossing, and then a rocky trail with poor overall footing. The most challenging section is, of course, near the top and is labeled "almost perpendicular" in quadrant A5 of the Trail Conference map. Close to the parking area you'll see several large boulders. I haven't clocked the top to bottom trip. But the reverse, the trip from the Johnsontown parking area to the top, takes 20 minutes.

This is the cave on the Doctors and Lawyers hike where the bandit Claudius Smith camped when he wasn't robbing and murdering.

If you want to see rabbits (or other wildlife) in Harriman Park, my advice is to visit around dusk in July.

TWIN PEAKS

DISTANCE: 5.0 Miles
TIME: 2.5 hours
DIFFICULTY LEVEL: Moderate
MAP: Harriman Bear Mountain Trails, northern, quadrants D2 and D3

Pros: two calendar quality views, easy to follow trails.

Cons: need to walk on paved road for a stretch, initial path is often flooded, one challenging scramble just before the top of Black Mountain.

Guiding Markers: Silvermine Lake, the overnight shelter, the lookout of Silvermine Lake, a sheer cliff face and stream, the Hudson River view, and Silvermine Ski trail.

Directions to Trailhead: From the intersection of Seven Lakes Dr. and Highway 17 North in Sloatsburg, follow Seven Lakes Dr. 7 miles and pull into the Silvermine Lake parking area. Several days a year the Park collects a fee for parking here.

DESCRIPTION

This moderate trek, which initially circles a lake, takes in two calendar quality views: one of Silvermine Lake, the other a broad sweep of The Hudson River. You can stop at the overnight shelter and read the logbook of the "through" hikers walking the length of the Appalachian trail. In the Spring to Fall season, its rather common to meet one of these adventurers in person. Except for one spot, the trails are well marked and the risk of getting lost is quite low.

ROUTE PLAN AND MARKING POSTS

Point A-Silvermine Lake parking area
Point B-Wm. Brien Memorial shelter

Walk toward Silvermine Lake and pick up the yellow (Menomine) trail behind a small shack. At first, the terrain is quite rocky. It's often flooded, so you may have to step on stone after stone to avoid getting wet. The trip around the edge of the lake takes 17 minutes. At the end of the lake, continue straight (do not take the road) on the yellow trail and after a steep 11 minute climb, you will be at the Wm. Brien Memorial shelter. The logbook makes interesting if not generally sophomoric reading. Most of the comments concern survival needs and functions. Through hikers generally adopt heroic monikers. You may also catch mention of bears raiding food at night.

Point B-Wm. Brien Memorial shelter
Point C-Silvermine Lookout

For this leg, you pick up the Applachian and Ramapo Dunderberg (white and red) trails, which run together. You can pick it up from one of two spots close to each other: just behind the shelter or about 25 yards east of the shelter. Continue on the doubly blazed white and red trails for about one mile. The terrain is pure woods with lots of large fields, and contains a mixture of slightly uphill, flat, and slightly downhill stretches. Eventually, you will reach a tremendous view of Silvermine Lake. I've tried many times but never snapped a really good photo here. The perspective that seems promising is to frame the lake between a tree and the trail.

Point C-Silvermine Lookout
Point D-Top of Black Mountain

Go another one-half mile on the Appalachian-Ramapo Dunderberg, passing, in this order, the Silvermine Ski Road, a towering cliff, one short scramble, and a stretch that goes along the edge of the mountain, to arrive at the flat plateau with a gorgeous view of the Hudson River. It takes searching, but a geological marker and the Spanish Mine are located nearby.

Point D-Top of Black Mountain
Point E-Seven Lakes Drive

Retrace your steps and at the base of the towering cliff head down the Silvermine Ski Road to Seven lakes Dr. This takes 20-30 minutes. At the end, watch for trails heading toward Seven Lakes Dr. You may miss them. Since you'll hear cars, break cross-country in the direction of the road for a short distance. This avoids walking in the wrong direction i.e. away from the parking lot.

Point E-Seven Lakes Drive
Point A-Silvermine Lake parking area

Go left (uphill) on Seven Lakes Dr. and in about 10 minutes you'll be at the parking area.

LAND AND LAKE

Distance: 4.5 miles
Time: 2 hours and 15 minutes
Difficulty Level: Easy +
Map: Harriman Bear Mountain Trails, southern, quadrant C4

Pros: An idyllic meadow view, mountain lakes, a short, fun cliff, a Hudson River lookout (best seen in winter), a charming old church with stained glass windows, hedges at the beginning give a feel of civilization vanishing in an instant.

Cons: no trespassing signs an eyesore, "threading" act required just before Third Reservoir due to convergence of trails.

Guiding Markers: bridge over stream in 10 minutes, paved road, Camp Lanowa on Breakneck Pond, Third Reservoir, Overnight Shelter atop Big Hill.

Directions to trail head: From Sloatsburg, take Seven Lakes Drive about 4 miles to Lake Welch Drive, bear right, continue 0.8 miles, and turn right onto an unmarked, paved road. About 200 yards ahead you'll see the Church's parking lot on your left.

DESCRIPTION

This relatively easy outing serves up a mixed concoction of three lakes balanced by deep quiet woods; the title is a play on the surf and turf specials at restaurants. At about the 10-minute mark, one stands on a bridge over a stream flowing out of a meadow. The scene is idyllic. It's worth a special trip, possibly for a less fit senior citizen. At the 25-minute mark, one stands on a rocky point jutting out into Breakneck Pond. This spot is also very beautiful. The Little Church in the Wilderness, a missionary church, built in the late

1800s, has a delightful country feel. My favorite stained glass window is the one closest to the entrance.

Point A-Church Parking Lot
Point B-Paved Road

Cross the road from the Church parking lot, walk about 20 feet toward Lake Welch or northwest, and then duck in. This is the path, shown on the Trail Conference Map as an unmarked trail. In about 30 yards, you'll be surrounded by tall hedges. The sense of being totally immersed in the forest is overwhelming. Civilization seems to have vanished. Continue mostly downhill on the modest grade, picking up the green (Long Path) trail in about five minutes. At the 10-minute mark, you'll reach a wood bridge over a stream flowing out of a meadow. This inspiring view melts troubles from your soul. I highly recommend it. Next, you'll pass a stand of fir trees on a plateau overlooking the meadow and then some apple trees before reaching a paved road. Do not turn left on the Long Path! More about this later on.

Point B-Paved road
Point C-Rocky Point in Breakneck Pond

Reaching the paved road, turn left and head towards Camp Lanowa; you'll pass a baseball field and a basketball court. After a short hill, you'll reach the camp with buildings and shelters on Breakneck Pond. This site is labeled "Camp Lanowa" on the Trail Conference map. (In the spring of 2006, I was told that the camp would be torn down. Since there were no campers this year, it seems likely that by the time this book is published the camp will have been demolished or another building erected at the site). At the very beginning of the camp, bear right on a dirt road for about 100 yards, cross over a small bridge, and then follow the dirt path to the rocky point extending into Breakneck Pond. If you walked to the other side of the lake, you missed the turn.

Point C-Rocky Point
Point D-Cabin 218

Retrace your steps to the paved road and then follow the dirt road around the other side of the lake, initially taking the road closest to the lake. Finding Cabin 218 is tricky; the landmarks are not distinctive. To orient, Cabin 218 is the very last shelter on the northwest end of the camp. It abuts the mountain's base and is set back from the lake.

Point D-Cabin 218
Point E-Third Reservoir

Behind cabin 218 a narrow unmarked trail climbs steeply up a short cliff. Some agility is required. Once at the top bear left onto the white or Breakneck Mountain trail. Here's the bad news: a small maze of trails converges at this point. Here's the good news: by just bearing left for less than 0.1 miles you should see Third Reservoir and be able to orient by sight. Hopefully, you've come across the yellow trail (Suffern Bear Mountain) and can descend to Third Reservoir. If not, orient visually and head for the lake.

Point E-Third Reservoir
Point F-Overnight Shelter

Now, turn left and walk along the perfectly flat—and this is no exaggeration-shore of Third Reservoir to Second reservoir. You'll pass an interesting mini park with a no trespassing sign. The town of Letchworth in Rockland County owns this land. They let you know it. Continue for another 0.25 miles before the end of Second Reservoir and you'll see an unamarked woods road heading into the woods. A guiding marker that tells you where to turn is, I believe, the third "no-trespassing" sign that has some red on it. After about 0.5 miles on this road, which at some points has been worn into small canyon by the rains, turn left on a stretch shared by the Long Path and Suffern Bear Mountain trails. This part is jointly blazed yellow and green. Your next step is a steep, 75-foot climb to the overnight shelter indicated by a "S" on the Trail Conference's map in quadrant D4. From this hill you can catch a glimpse of the Hudson River; its not a great view, especially in the summer when trees obstruct the panorama. In September 2006, I came across a 10-year-old boy camping with his family near the shelter who was thrilled that he had found some snakeskin. Here's where my narrow focus on nature photography was limited, because the look on the boy's face, if accurately rendered, could have appeared in Life magazine.

Point F-Overnight shelter
Point G-Church Parking Lot

The way back is easy. Continue on the blue (Long Path) 150 yards to the Old Turnpike, turn left, and retrace your steps to the paved road that leads to the bridge at the edge of the meadow on the initial trip. Note there is an alternative route back. It is not recommended!!!! Instead of the Old Turnpike, you could take the Long Path through the woods. I have no details. But every nerve in my body says that something gruesome happened here once. I had terrible dreams the night after walking here. Christine B. felt the same dread. My guess is that there is an Indian burial ground along this stretch. I'm not alone is noticing creepy places. The October 2006 issue of the Appalachian Mountain Club's magazine contained an article that profiled six scary spots in New England.

I love the stained glass windows at this country church.

It's hard to get a good shot of a woodchuck. They must have a keen sense of smell.

THE WONDERS OF NATURE

Distance: 5.5 miles
Time: 2.5 hours
Difficulty Level: Moderate
Map: Harriman Bear Mountain Trails, Southern, quadrant A5

Pros: incredible scenic variety, nice waterfalls, good panorama from the top of North Mountain, two optional detours to good lookouts, stream conducive to quiet reflection (Walden Pond-like).

Cons: view southwest at one point on the optional extension marred by power station, muddy spots, very steep initial ascent, white trail hard to follow at about the half-mile point.

Guiding Markers: Reeves Meadow Brook, a series of waterfalls, an elevated promontory-like rock formation, the base of a steep cliff, the top of North Mountain, a power station, a flat open area at the base of the mountain, a large meadow, a stream bed, a stand of tall pine trees.

Directions to trailhead: From the intersection of Route 17 and Seven Lakes Dr., follow Seven Lakes Dr. east under the Thruway overpass for about 1.5 miles. Park at the Visitor Center on your right.

DESCRIPTION

This full circle outing contains three separate and distinct hikes. In this first section, one is dazzled by series of closely spaced waterfalls and what seems like nature's calculated display of variety-a hollow, a marsh, an open brushy area, and a sheer precipice. In the second leg, the trek rings around the summit of North Mountain, affording panoramic views, and then traces a V-pattern, plunging into a valley and coming up the other side. The last segment, which is mostly level, passes a charming stream, a boulder-filled stream bed, and a grove of fir trees.

ROUTE PLAN AND MARKING POSTS

Point A-Visitor Center on Seven Lakes Drive
Point B-Small Crag

Head east about 50 yards toward the stream on the red (Pine Meadow) trail to meet up with the white (Reeves Brook) trail on your right. The next mile, a virtual microcosm of Harriman Park, contains amazing diversity: a fern glade, a series of small and medium sized waterfalls, an open brushy area, a marsh, a hollow, and a small crag. Several notes to keep in mind: the initial climb is the steepest, bear left at a fork between a road and the white trail, and the last two waterfalls are the best. In my opinion, the mini cliff (point B) looks more like a "speaking platform" where an orator might address crowds than the flat area in quadrant B6 labeled "the pulpit" on the Trail Conference's map.

At the risk of sounding Jungian or "New Age," I'm going to state for the record that this path possess a unique feel: a clear, tingly pleasurable sensation. This was my favorite walk for months. I can't be sure, but it feels like pheromones between man and nature. The fact that the trail parallels a fault line could be a more western explanation for the effect exerted by this section of what one friend calls "the enchanted trail."

Point B-Small Crag
Point C-Intersection of blue (Seven Hills) trail

This one-half mile stretch follows Reeves Brook at first and then strays a bit west, passing a small bog and a flat boulder split down the center before reaching the Seven Hills (blue) trail. Across or north from this point towers a large granite cliff about 100 ft. high. I recommend the climb as a detour. It's challenging, somewhat acrobatic, and makes you feel like an explorer. The view on top is quite good.

Point C Intersection of blue (Seven Hills) trail
Point D-Top of North Hill

This 15-minute stretch passes relatively non-descript territory before starting a modest climb to the summit of North Mountain. Kudos to the original trailblazer! The skillfully designed Seven Hills trail rings around the mountains' top, capturing the full panorama. Several flat granite perches look out toward the horizon and serve as excellent possible lunch stops.

Point D-Top of North Hill
Point E-Intersection of Orange (Hillburn-Torne-Sebago) trail

You now trace a V-pattern, descending steeply between two peaks before climbing the other side. The down section is generally over smooth granite; the climb is over a boulder field. Once you reach the other side look back. Immediately behind you is a neat view of two mountains. Unfortunately … looking southwest you'll glimpse a power plant, an ugly reminder of civilization.

Point E-Intersection of Orange (H-T-S) Trail
Point F-Base of hill

Continuing on the blue trail, walk along a plateau area before descending about 175 ft. to the base of the mountain. (Before doing this, you'll have the option of following the orange trail to the Ramapo Torne, which overlooks Highway 17 and Sharp Plaza). At the base you'll notice a flat, mostly cleared area bordered by a small stream. I always sensed something here-a mine, a building, etc. but never discovered anything.

Point F-Base of hill
Point A-Visitor Center on Seven Lakes Drive

The 1.5-mile section contains many flat sections; on balance, the total elevation gain is probably less than 50 feet. A stream at about the ¼ mile mark coming down from a steep angle off the mountain is particularly inspiring. I feel it has Walden Pond-like qualities. If you have the time, try to rest here for a few moments to take it in. Since the creek runs even during the summer, albeit at a reduced level, it probably draws from a source other than rainwater. What is its benefactor? Maybe an underground formation higher up on the mountain traps water? The next major attraction on this stretch about ½ mile ahead is a boulder filled stream-bed and shortly beyond that (about one-quarter of a mile from Seven Lakes Dr.), a stand of tall fir trees. Turn right onto the red trail just after you hear cars and you'll see the visitor center in a few minutes. Various insects, including giant bumble bees, inhabit the meadow adjacent to the parking area in the summer months.

This bush was apparently a "United Nations" for insects with a bumble bee, a cricket, a wasp, and a butterfly present for roll call.

An old rock's snow hat begins to melt in late winter.

TASTING THE HIGH COUNTRY

DISTANCE: 5.5 miles
TIME: 2 hours, 30 minutes
DIFFICULTY LEVEL: Moderate
MAP: Harriman Park Bear Mountain Trails, southern, quadrant B5

Pros: at least four cliffs, a delightful view of Lake Sebago, a "sneak peak" at Lake Wanoksink on the eastern side of the range, large boulders, "sky ponds" on the top of the ridge after a rain, pine trees.

Cons: Slight overlap or double counting in routes, part of the trail on the ridge is obscured by brush, several tricky scrambles, need to exercise extreme caution near the cliffs.

Guiding Markers: a stream, large boulders, the view of Lake Sebago, the intersection of the Seven Hills and the HTS trails, the cliff views, Pine Meadow Lake, a sign that says "Hikers Please Walk in Ski Tracks."

Directions to Trailhead: From the intersection of Highway 17 and Seven Lakes Dr., follow Seven Lakes Drive east about 3 miles and turn left into the area marked "Boat Basin." Park at the edge of Lake Sebago.

DESCRIPTION

This hike's central attraction is a series of about four closely spaced cliffs along a stretch of the blue-blazed Seven Hills trail. This is exciting terrain and, to the best of my knowledge, unique in Harriman Park. The last and scariest precipice plunges a knife-edge 75 ft. straight down. Stay away from the edge! Repeat: stay away from the edge. Harriman Park is not Yosemite. But for the New York metropolitan area the phrase "high country" in the hike's title fits. A second feature is an absorbing view of Lake Sebago. This straight-on look at

Harriman's Park's second largest lake has an encompassing, center stage quality. It certainly ranks in Harriman's top five. There's also a pleasing lookout of Lake Wanoksink. In conceptualizing this trek, organize your thoughts around the ridge running along the top of Diamond Mountain. (In fact, the hike could be subtitled "The Great Divide") On one side of the ridge facing west is the view of Lake Sebago; and on the other side, facing east, are the four-plus cliff lookouts.

ROUTE PLAN AND MARKING POSTS (Segments A to E)

Point A-Sebago Boat Launch Parking Area
Point B-View of Lake Sebago in quadrant B5

This 45-minute leg on one trail, the blue-blazed Seven Hills trail, breaks down into two main parts: the steep initial climb, and then, after the trail changes direction, a walk along the ridge. The initial climb from Seven Lakes Dr. to a plateau takes about ten minutes. The climb is easier if you walk on the shoulder instead of in the channel. From the plateau, you'll dip down to a stream, and then climb another minute to the point where the blue trail breaks off southwest (right) at almost a 90-degree angle. From here, it takes about 35 minutes to reach the view indicated as a star in quadrant B5 of the Trail Conference's map. As indicated earlier, this view is a crowd pleaser, one of Harriman's Park's best. One charm of the ridge walk itself are a few large boulders (glacial erratics); they seemed to roll to the edge of the mountain and stop; just a few more feet and it would have been, "look out below." The largest boulder stands an estimated 25 ft. high.

Point B-view of Lake Sebago
Point C-Ridge Bluff

This 12-minute section passes some depressions or sky ponds if it's rained recently and at about the halfway mark is jointly blazed orange and blue. You won't be able to miss the signs for the intersection of the blue Seven Hills and orange Hillburn-Torne-Sebago routes. It's been spray-painted onto rock in bright colors. Less than 100 yards ahead is an area, which is effectively the end of the ridge. There's a neat overlook here, both down the valley, and directly east at the other mountain, which has a clearing or bald spot.

Point C-Ridge Bluff
Point D-Pine Meadow Brook

This section is action-packed. About 45 ft down from the ridge bluff on the blue trail and after a scramble, head left off trail on a flat rock for some 25 yards. There you'll spot Lake Wanoksink to the northeast. It feels like a "sneak peak" or a "discovery." Return to the trail to negotiate a steep, sideways slanted area where it's necessary to crab on all fours. In about 20 minutes you'll reach "cliff row." On July 15, 2006, I counted at least four crag turnouts (all to the right).

Lookout no. 1 is mainly a collection of boulders and has a nice "tunnel" or "barrel" type view down the valley towards the Visitor Center; each lookout shares this "telescopic" feature. Lookout no. 2 features a sheer 25 ft. drop. Lookout no. 3 has one large boulder and is not as exciting. Lookout no. 4 drops off 34-45 feet and is scary. The last lookout, announced by four 14-18 ft. pine trees, is absolutely terrifying! The fear factor comes from both the 75-ft. free fall and the flat, deceptively safe granite ledge that borders the cliff. Stay away from the edge! Also, avoid watching Alfred Hitchcock movies afterwards! (Note that if you venture north to the Shawangunks near New Paltz, NY sheer drops are common.) Finally, on the way down to the base of Diamond Mountain there's twisting turns and a three ft. step down before you reach Pine Meadow Brook in the valley. This route could be challenging for a child. Once down, try to turn around and look back. You'll see a cliff, with a tapering outline reminiscent of Half Dome.

Point D-Pine Meadow Brook
Point E-Ski Tracks Sign

Follow the red (Pine Meadow) trail west along a stream toward Pine Meadow Lake, passing first a wood bridge on your right, and then Ga Nus Quah, the stone giants, in quadrant B5. About 100 yards before the lake, turn left onto a wide woods road and continue for about ½ mile. Its not likely, but you may see cars. Two bonus attractions in about 10 minutes when you reach a small stone bridge: (1) a 50-ft waterslide east of the bridge, and (2) at the northeast corner of the meadow, a small waterfall. One of the happiest moments in my long hiking career was observing the sheer volume generated by this waterslide after a several days of heavy rain. In some ways it was more beautiful than an actual waterfall. Lake Wanoksink is less than 100 yards away. Sometimes I'll head up there to photograph the flowers in the early summer, pick blue berries in July, or look for beavers swimming in the lake in winter.

Point E-Ski Tracks Sign
Point A-Sebago Boat Launch Parking Area

Turn left at the sign that reads "Hikers Please Walk in Ski Tracks" and take the bare, right most dirt road. Do not take the grass-covered dirt road on the left. You'll now climb a small hill. At the top, you'll pass the red-blazed Tuxedo-Mt. Ivy trail, and then descend to the stream you crossed earlier in the day. There are several very smooth rock surfaces here, which raise the risk of a fall or slip, particularly in the winter, so I recommend walking on the dirt trail.

Be careful! Just behind this plateau on the Tasting High Country hike is a sheer cliff. Pine trees tend to be found near cliffs in Harriman Park.

EXTRAS

The following short pieces are extracts from the larger and more comprehensive version of this book, as originally conceived, and are intended to illustrate how a day in Harriman Park can be a virtual "One Day Vacation." Topics covered include where to dine, wildlife sightings, my wildlife log for one day, where to take a great fall foliage picture, a perfect hideaway, a movie theatre recommendation, and homespun foot care advice.

CHICKEN SOUP AND OTHER DISHES TO CAP THE DAY

The chicken soup at Hacienda de Don Manuel (located at 72 Lafayette St. in Suffern, NY) is more than a delicious broth filled with chunks of white meat chicken, carrots, and turnips—it's a tonic, and a completely filling one at that. It's the perfect climax to a day filled with sun, hiking and outdoor adventures. A cup for lunch costs $3.75 as of September 2006. One caution of a historical note: the quality of the soup deteriorated considerably after the restaurant moved from a previous location 100 yards away, also on Lafayette St., in 2004. In fact, I stopped frequenting the establishment. However, after giving them a second chance in August 2006, I was pleasantly surprised to taste the familiar and delicious broth once again.

The Olde Towne Inne located at 116 Orange Ave, Suffern, NY 10901 (845-369-3999) directly across from the train station makes a tasty turkey club sandwich that comes with homemade chips that costs $7.95 as of October 2006. The restaurant's signature dish is Chicken Kowloon that goes for $14.95 on the dinner menu. Quoting from the actual menu, this entre is made of "breaded Rolla tines of chicken rolled with savory seafood stuffing, topped with a creamy mushroom sauce." The dish comes with bread, salad, rice pilaf and a vegetable. Most of the restaurants other offerings are prepared by Chef James in a low calorie manner.

Pasta Cuchina located at 8 Airmont Rd. in Suffern, NY 10901 (845-369-1313, www.pastacucina.com) is an Italian restaurant serving Suffern, New City and Stony Point. It has good prices, tasty concoctions, large crowds, and friendly service. Think of it as a more modern, suburban Carmine's (an old New York Italian restaurant famous for its large portions).The early bird special is a fantastic deal. For $10.95 you get bread, salad, a choice of entrees (cavatelli and brocoli, shrimp scampi, chicken parmagiana, daily seafood, etc.), desert, and coffee or tea. Desert choices include crisp Italian cannoli, New York cheesecake, and Tartofo Supreme. The promotional is offered between 3 and 5 PM Monday to Thursday.

GOSLINGS COME OUT IN THE SPRING

Straight out of a Dr. Seuss book, these small, furry, yellow goslings (young geese) appear like clockwork in early May in areas close to water. Four such spots where you are likely to encounter these birds are: The Lake Kanawauke Circle on Seven Lakes Drive, the shore of Lake Skanattiti about 0.5 miles east of the Kanawauke Circle, the western edge of Lake Tiorati across from the campground, and on the Bear Mountain Side of the Park, at Iona Island. Try to arrive in the mornings between 8:30 and 11:00 on clear days, and the odds are quite high you will spot four to six of these diminutive birds accompanied by one or both parents. The goslings sprout fast, so if you wait until late May, they'll already be in their adolescent stage, and their appearance will be distinctly darker, and scragglier than the cute babies.

FALL FOLIAGE PHOTO

Timing and clear weather are key. Wait for peak foliage, generally the second or third week in October. As soon as it's bright enough, climb to the top of the lookout marked by a * in quadrant C4 of the Southern Harriman Park map on the red Arden Surebridge Trail. Your starting point will be the parking lot alongside Lake Skannatati just off Seven Lakes Drive. This climb will take about 10 minutes and involve one scramble. Take my word for it—you'll capture a memorable shot. Lake Kanawauke, which lies straight ahead, will register as a shimmering blue mirror. A yellow patch of foliage on the right provides a contrasting accent. What's more, nature seems to encourage picture taking from this spot. Just above a short rise behind the actual lookout are two trees that perfectly frame the overlook, giving the shot a professional-quality finish. For another interesting artistic effect, try putting rocks in the foreground.

PICNIC SPOT AND CLIFF CLIMB

Harriman's version of The Plaza Hotel, this picnic ledge has amenities (privacy, shelter from the wind, level ground, and a campfire site) that would impress even the most jaded traveler. This challenging climb is only recommended for advanced hikers in excellent physical shape. Getting there takes about 20 minutes from the Lake Skannatati Parking Lot. Follow the blue trail (long path) around the lake for about ½ mile. Cross the stream at the edge of the lake, then go another 0.25 mile and stop at the 45-ft. rock face on the right. You'll hear a voice. It's not the wind. It's the cliff saying, "climb me, climb me." Depending on your ability and comfort level, you can now either climb this edifice or walk around the back. Slithering front first on your belly seems to work best for a spot about 70% the way up. Once on top, walk 100 yards to your left through brush until you reach this comfortable, hidden cove.

FOOT INSOLES

One should always consult a qualified medical professional in important health matters. In fact, there are many different options for arch support and foot cushioning which you should investigate. A podiatrist working the USA Today 800 number once gave me sage advice for plantar nerve pain—Spenco ¾ length orthotic arch supports. He was quite adamant in emphasizing the particular the brand and model. He didn't seem to have any marketing axe to grind. It was great advice. Besides alleviating my plantar faciitis, I discovered these pads (which have green cushions and hard black plastic under soles) are an improvement over the insoles that ordinarily come with hiking boots and great for tired feet. I wear them all the time! One merchant in Montclair, NJ sells them for around $25.

SEE A MOVIE AT THE LAFAYETTE THEATRE

About 12 years ago the Wall Street Journal highlighted a magnificent old movie theatre in Oakland, Calif. A runner up might be the Lafayette Theatre in Suffern, NY. Built in 1909 and in recent years revitalized by a local family, this large, single-screen theatre has the charm and comfort of yesteryear's grand cinema houses. For Manhattanites, its soooo comfortable to have spacious seats and not have people hogging the arm rest. An old Wurlitzer jukebox adds to the sense of being in a time warp. Here's the website and phone number:

www.bigscreenclassics.com, 845-369-8234. Address: 97 Lafayette St, Suffern, NY 10901.

WILDLIFE SIGHTS FOR ONE SAMPLE DAY

My wildlife log for Friday, November 21, 2003, is replete with entries. Driving west on Lake Welch Drive around dusk, I counted a total of 14 deer within 10 feet of the road. Most were feeding outside a meadow behind The Little Church in the Wilderness. Surprisingly, several of the animals at one point raced down the road heading in the same direction as the cars. Were they confused, thinking that the road was their personal trail? A few of the mammals were bucks with antlers, clad in thick winter fur. Just past Lake Sebago on Seven Lakes Drive, a brown, medium-sized, rodent poked his head out at one point. My guess is that the creature was a woodchuck or a beaver, although it could have been something else e.g. a possum. Earlier, I noticed a flock of black crows gathered along Seven Lakes Drive They appeared to be feeding, but I could not tell what their sustenance was. During the walk to the top of West Mountain, squirrels scampered on the ground, and then leaped to safety in the trees. On top of the mountain, hawks were visible, circling at high altitudes. Just off the bike trail from the Anthony Wayne Parking Lot on the return trip, I spotted a bird's nest in a fallen tree. In the early summer of 2004, I had been astonished to find an exposed and vulnerable bird's nest containing eggs three feet off the ground at the base of a cliff on the Tuxedo-Mt. Ivy trail. I attempted to duplicate this sighting in 2005 but was not successful. The bird must have gotten smarter.

978-0-595-42100-8
0-595-42100-8

Made in the USA
Middletown, DE
26 June 2015